A...
Le...ie value: 550

# COWS
## Don't Live In
# TREES!

## SUPER SCIENCE

CLARA MACCARALD

Rourke
Educational Media
rourkeeducationalmedia.com

A Division of
Carson
Dellosa
Education

## Before Reading: *Building Background Knowledge and Vocabulary*

Building background knowledge can help children process new information and build upon what they already know. Before reading a book, it is important to tap into what children already know about the topic. This will help them develop their vocabulary and increase their reading comprehension.

### Questions and Activities to Build Background Knowledge:

1. Look at the front cover of the book and read the title. What do you think this book will be about?
2. What do you already know about this topic?
3. Take a book walk and skim the pages. Look at the table of contents, photographs, captions, and bold words. Did these text features give you any information or predictions about what you will read in this book?

### Vocabulary: *Vocabulary Is Key to Reading Comprehension*

Use the following directions to prompt a conversation about each word.

- Read the vocabulary words.
- What comes to mind when you see each word?
- What do you think each word means?

**Vocabulary Words:**
- amphibians
- bamboo
- gills
- grasslands
- habitat
- prey
- thorns
- tropics

## During Reading: *Reading for Meaning and Understanding*

To achieve deep comprehension of a book, children are encouraged to use close reading strategies. During reading, it is important to have children stop and make connections. These connections result in deeper analysis and understanding of a book.

 Close Reading a Text

During reading, have children stop and talk about the following:

- Any confusing parts
- Any unknown words
- Text to text, text to self, text to world connections
- The main idea in each chapter or heading

Encourage children to use context clues to determine the meaning of any unknown words. These strategies will help children learn to analyze the text more thoroughly as they read.

When you are finished reading this book, turn to the next-to-last page for **Text-Dependent Questions** and an **Extension Activity**.

# TABLE OF CONTENTS

COWS DON'T CLIMB!................ 4

DO BEARS EAT TREES?............. 9

DO LIZARDS LIVE
AT THE SOUTH POLE?............. 14

SLOTHS DON'T POOP IN TREES!.... 18

ACTIVITY...................... 21

GLOSSARY...................... 22

INDEX......................... 23

TEXT-DEPENDENT QUESTIONS....... 23

EXTENSION ACTIVITY............ 23

ABOUT THE AUTHOR.............. 24

# COWS DON'T CLIMB!

Imagine going to a farm. Where will you look for a cow? Not in a tree! But why not?

Cows can't climb trees. They don't have the right kind of legs. Plus, they mostly eat things low to the ground like grass.

**Tree Goats**
Goats eat just about anything. And they can climb. Some goats spend time in trees. Watch out below!

Just like a cow, every kind of animal lives in a special place. An animal's place is called its **habitat**. Habitats have the things that animals need.

All animals need different things. They eat different things. They survive different kinds of weather. You wouldn't expect an elephant to live in the same place as a polar bear!

**The Icy North**
Polar bears roam sea ice to hunt. Seals have trouble seeing them because the bears' coats blend in with the ice.

Habitats can be places such as deserts, **grasslands**, or lakes. They might be as large as a forest or as small as a tree. A crow on a farm doesn't live in the exact same habitat as a cow on that same farm.

**Lunch on the Go**
A tick might live for days on a deer. While the deer roams the forest, the tick drinks its blood.

# DO BEARS EAT TREES?

All animals need food. Animals must live in habitats that have the kinds of food they eat. Plant-eaters live where they can find the plants they like. Predators live near their **prey**.

*Pelicans nest on islands, staying close to the fish they eat.*

**Picky Koalas**
Koalas almost always eat gum tree leaves, so they live in gum trees. Dinner is only a short climb away!

Some animals eat only a few things, or even just one thing. What if you could only eat pizza for the rest of your life? You'd probably want to live next to a pizza restaurant!

Panda bears eat **bamboo** and almost nothing else. Panda bears can only live in bamboo forests. They'd go hungry anywhere else.

Black bears eat many things. They snack on fruit. They catch fish. They eat a few larger animals that don't escape them fast enough.

Black bears live in many places. You can find black bears in forests, grasslands, and deserts. Black bears even climb trees to look for snacks. But you won't see a black bear climbing a cactus. Ouch!

**Black Bear Nests?**
Many black bears spend the winter in dens. But people have seen some bears spending the winter in eagle nests!

bear den

# DO LIZARDS LIVE AT THE SOUTH POLE?

A pet lizard might wear a sweater. But wild lizards have neither wool nor fur to fight off the cold. You wouldn't expect to see a lizard in the coldest places on Earth. A lizard at the South Pole would become an ice pop!

**Frog Pops**
Wood frogs can freeze. They spend the winter as blocks of ice. In the spring, they melt and hop away!

Some reptiles and **amphibians** live in habitats with warm summers and cold winters. They can't fly away for the winter, like birds do. Instead, many spend the winter underground where it's warmer. They hibernate as they wait for the spring.

Some animals don't want to be very warm. A furry yak would get too hot in the **tropics**!

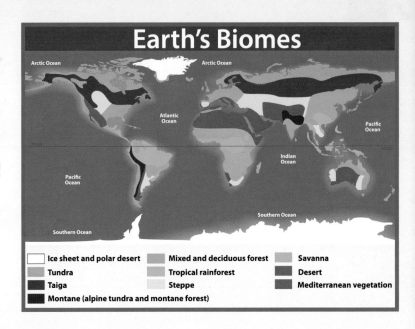

## Earth's Biomes

| | | |
|---|---|---|
| ☐ Ice sheet and polar desert | Mixed and deciduous forest | Savanna |
| Tundra | Tropical rainforest | Desert |
| Taiga | Steppe | Mediterranean vegetation |
| Montane (alpine tundra and montane forest) | | |

*Wild yaks live in cold grasslands and deserts. Some live in a tree-less land called the tundra.*

**Fish Out of Water**
Walking catfish can breathe air. They use stiff fins to cross over land while looking for a new lake.

Animals need to avoid freezing or frying. They also need to breathe. Land animals breathe air. Fish breathe through **gills**. Most fish can't breathe without water. Fish would also dry out on land.

You wouldn't expect to see a shark crawling through a forest. Or to find a deer deep in the ocean!

17

# SLOTHS DON'T POOP IN TREES!

Animals need to eat. They also need to avoid being eaten. A good way to stay safe is to live in the right habitat.

Some insects look like leaves. They must live on or near plants. They'd be easy to see if they lived on a sandy beach!

*In addition to leaves, insects might look like sticks, flowers, or even bird poop.*

**City Living**
Deer love city parks and yards. They have to watch out for cars, but at least there aren't any wolves!

Prey animals need places to hide. Rabbits like having thick plants to duck under. Squirrels need trees to race up. They use leaves and sticks to make nests to hide in.

Many birds nest in trees. Leaves make the nests hard to see. In the desert, some birds nest in cactuses. Anyone trying to eat them might get a mouthful of **thorns**!

*Some doves eat cactus fruit. These doves are nesting as close as they can to their food source!*

Sloths are prey animals. They move very slowly. Predators would find them easy to catch on the ground. Sloths only go to the ground to poop. They spend the rest of their time in trees, staying safe and eating leaves. Sloths are like cows that live in trees!

# ACTIVITY

## Make a Habitat

Learn more about an animal by making its habitat in a box.

## Supplies

- shoebox or other box
- scissors
- glue or tape
- art materials: colored paper, markers, craft sticks, bark, grass, cotton, clay, small toys, or anything else you have on hand
- books or websites about animal and their habitats

## Directions

1. Choose an animal. Use the art materials to make the animal or use a toy animal. Place it in the box.

2. Find books or websites about your animal. Where does the animal live? What does it eat? Does it have predators it must hide from?

3. Make a habitat for your animal. Using your supplies, make food, water, and shelter for your animal. You can make trees, bushes, lakes, or anything else you want. Tape or glue these to the sides of your box or make them stick up from the bottom.

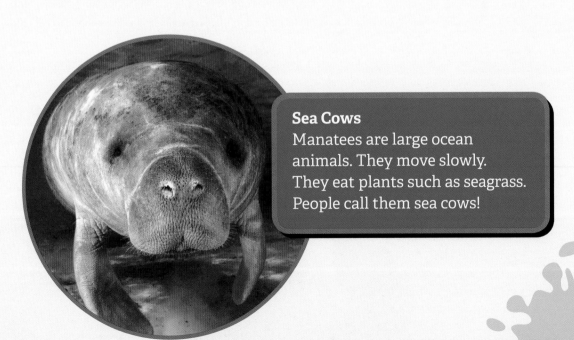

**Sea Cows**
Manatees are large ocean animals. They move slowly. They eat plants such as seagrass. People call them sea cows!

# GLOSSARY

**amphibians** (am-FIB-ee-uhns): cold-blooded animals with backbones that live in the water when young; frogs and toads are amphibians

**bamboo** (bam-BOO): a wood-like grass with a hollow stem

**gills** (gils): the parts on each side of a fish's mouth that allow it to breathe underwater

**grasslands** (GRAS-lands): large, open areas covered with grass

**habitat** (HAB-i-tat): a place where an animal or plant lives

**prey** (pray): an animal that is hunted by another animal

**thorns** (thorns): sharp points sticking off a plant

**tropics** (TRAH-piks): very hot parts of Earth that get a lot of sun

# INDEX

bear(s) 7, 11, 12, 13

cactus(es) 13, 19

cow(s) 4, 6, 8, 20

deer 8, 17, 18

fish 9, 12, 17

lizard(s) 14

nest(s) 9, 13, 19

sloths 18, 20

# TEXT-DEPENDENT QUESTIONS

1. How do reptiles survive a cold winter?

2. What do panda bears eat?

3. Why do squirrels make nests?

4. Why do sloths live in trees?

5. What makes a cactus a good place for a bird nest?

# EXTENSION ACTIVITY

Visit a habitat. It can be big or small. It can be in the country or in a city. Write down the names of animals you find there. Can you guess why they are where they are? Look for books that tell you more about these animals. What do they eat? What eats them? Do they like to be very cold or very warm? Do they live in other habitats besides the one you found them in? Write a little bit about each animal you see.

# ABOUT THE AUTHOR

Clara MacCarald lives in a forest in New York with her family and all the pets she didn't have as a kid (four cats and two dogs). She writes books for kids in subjects such as science and history. Some of her books are out of this world—a couple of them are about Mars! When not writing, she can be found holding woolly bear caterpillars with her daughter or herding toads off the driveway.

www.rourkeeducationalmedia.com

PHOTO CREDITS: Cover, page 1: ©Acisak Mitrprayoon; page 3: ©Lalocracio; page 4: ©VLIET; page 5: ©republica; page 6: ©1001slide; page 7: ©Matt Pain; page 8: ©UrosPoteko; page 8b: ©Antagain; page 9: ©Richard Constantinoff; page 10: ©Dirk Freder; page 11: ©powerofforever; page 12: ©Sherran L. Pratt; page 13a: ©blazer76; page 13b: ©Lynn_Bystrom; page 14-15: ©dlewis33; page 14: ©Werner Schneider; page 16: ©Davor Lovincic; page 16b: ©ttsz; page 17: ©RamonCarretero; page 18a: ©SHAWSHANK61; page 18b: ©Winhorse; page 19: ©vivavado; page 20: ©Mikelane55; page 21: ©Amanda Cotton; page 22: ©Daniel Prudek

Edited by: Kim Thompson
Cover and interior design by: Rhea Magaro-Wallace

**Library of Congress PCN Data**

Cows Don't Live in Trees! / Clara MacCarald
(Super Science)
  ISBN 978-1-73161-436-0 (hard cover)
  ISBN 978-1-73161-231-1 (soft cover)
  ISBN 978-1-73161-541-1 (e-Book)
  ISBN 978-1-73161-646-3 (ePub)
Library of Congress Control Number: 2019932078

Rourke Educational Media
Printed in the United States of America,
North Mankato, Minnesota